FATE™
ACCELERATED

CLARK VALENTINE
WRITING • REFINEMENT

LEONARD BALSERA
CORE SYSTEM DEVELOPMENT

FRED HICKS
CONCEPT • WRITING • LAYOUT

MIKE OLSON
SYSTEM EDITING

AMANDA VALENTINE
CLARITY • EDITING

CLAUDIA CANGINI
COVER ART • INTERIOR ART

FATE WAS ORIGINALLY CREATED BY

ROB DONOGHUE AND FRED HICKS

EVIL HAT
PRODUCTIONS

An Evil Hat Productions Publication
www.evilhat.com • feedback@evilhat.com
@EvilHatOfficial on Twitter
facebook.com/EvilHatProductions

Fate Accelerated Edition
Copyright © 2013 Evil Hat Productions, LLC.
All rights reserved.

First published in 2013 by Evil Hat Productions, LLC.
10125 Colesville Rd #318, Silver Spring, MD 20901.

Softcover ISBN: 978-1-61317-047-2
Kindle ISBN: 978-1-61317-055-7
ePub ISBN: 978-1-61317-054-0

Printed in the USA

This is a game where people make up stories about wonderful, terrible, impossible,
glorious things. All the characters and events portrayed in this work are fictional.
Any resemblance to real people, magical martial artists, schoolgirl witches,
pulp scientists, or piratical cats is purely coincidental, but kinda hilarious.

CONTENTS

GET STARTED!

Remember those books where the teenage wizards struggle against the Dark Lord of Evil? That movie where the dwarves fight to recapture their mountain home from a dragon? That animated TV show about mystical knights and their army of clones righting wrongs across the galaxy?

Aren't those *awesome*?

Here's your chance to put yourself in the heroes' shoes in stories like those.

Fate Accelerated Edition is a tabletop roleplaying game, where you and your friends gather around and tell stories full of danger, excitement, and adventure. You might have played games similar to this before—*Dungeons & Dragons* is a very popular one—but don't worry if you haven't; this booklet will guide you through it.

Here's what you'll need to play:

- **Three to five people.** One of you will be the **gamemaster**, the others **players**. We'll talk about what those mean later.

- **Fate Dice™**, at least four, preferably four per person. These are a special kind of six-sided dice that are marked on two sides with a plus symbol (➕), two sides with a minus symbol (➖), and two sides are blank (⬛). You can get these dice from many hobby and game stores, often under their original name—Fudge dice. We call them Fate Dice in this book, but you can call them whatever you like. Evil Hat will offer Fate Dice for sale at *www.evilhat.com* later in 2013.

  > If you don't want to use Fudge dice, you don't have to—any set of regular six-sided dice will work. If you're using regular dice, you read 5 or 6 as ➕, 1 or 2 as ➖, and 3 or 4 as ⬛.

- The **Deck of Fate** is an alternative to Fate Dice. It's a deck of cards that mimics the probability of Fate Dice, and it's designed to be used in the same way Fate Dice are. The Deck of Fate will be available from Evil Hat in 2013 or 2014.

- **Character sheets**, one for each player. You can download these from *www.evilhat.com*.

- **Index cards** or **sticky notes** or similar slips of paper.

- **Tokens for fate points**. These can be poker chips, beads, pennies, or anything similar. Get a handful—about 30 or 40.

Next, let's talk about how to use *Fate Accelerated* to tell stories together.

TELLING STORIES TOGETHER

So you've gathered your friends, your dice, and your index cards, and you're ready to play *Fate Accelerated Edition* (we'll call it *FAE* from now on). Time to tell some stories!

WHAT DO YOU MEAN, "TELL STORIES"?

FAE is all about telling stories. You create a group of characters and follow them through some imaginary adventure that you all take turns telling little parts of.

Think about a movie, video game, or TV show you like where the characters go on adventures—something like *The Legend of Korra* or *Star Wars* or *The Avengers* or the *Zelda* games or *Doctor Who* or *The Lord of the Rings*. Now imagine a similar sort of story, where you and your friends around the table make the decisions for the characters as they move through the story, and the story changes as you make those decisions.

Sometimes someone makes a decision to try something and you don't know for sure how it would turn out; that's when you roll dice to see what happens next. The higher you roll, the better the chance that things work out the way you want them to.

SO HOW DO WE DO IT?

Well, first you need to figure out what kind of story you're going to tell. What genre are you interested in? Fantasy? Science fiction? Modern-day adventure? Will you play in the world of a TV show or comic book or movie that you love, or will you create your own world? For some great advice about how to design the framework of your game, see *Game Creation* in *Fate Core*, available for free at *www.evilhat.com*.

Next, it's time to choose who will be the players, and who will be the gamemaster. Of the people around the table, all but one are referred to as **players**. Each player takes on the role of one **player character** or **PC** in the story, and puts themselves in their character's shoes to make the decisions that their character would make. The remaining person is called the **game-master** or **GM**. The GM's job is to present challenges to the players and to portray all the characters that aren't controlled by the players (**non-player characters** or **NPCs**).

More on the the GM's job: p. 35

Once you decide who the GM will be, and what the genre and framework of the story will be, it's time for the players to make their characters—that's in the next chapter.

Who do you want to be? p. 8

TELLING STORIES "TOGETHER"?
WHAT DO YOU MEAN?

All the people at the table, GM and players alike, are responsible for telling the story. When you make a decision for your character (or for one of the NPCs, if you're the GM), think about two things.

First, put yourself in your character's shoes and think hard about what they would do—even if it's not the best idea. If you're playing a character that sometimes makes poor decisions, don't be afraid to make a poor decision for them on purpose.

Second—and this is really important—think about the story that's being told. Think about the choice that would make that story even better: more interesting, more exciting, funnier. Would a certain choice give another player's character a chance to be awesome? Strongly consider making that choice.

That's how you tell great stories *together*—by not being afraid for your character to make mistakes, and by making choices that make the story more interesting for everyone at the table—not just you.

TELLING STORIES TOGETHER

WHO DO YOU WANT TO BE?

Once you've decided what kind of story you'll be telling in your game, you decide who your character is—what they look like, what they're good at, and what they believe.

WHAT KIND OF CHARACTERS CAN I PLAY?

Think about the setting that you've decided to play in and make that your main guide. Are you playing in a school for young sorcerers? Play a young sorcerer! Are you playing space pilots fighting an evil empire? Play a space pilot! Make sure your character has a reason to interact and cooperate with the characters the other players are making.

HOW DO I MAKE THE CHARACTER?

Now it's time to start writing stuff down. Grab a pencil and a copy of the character sheet. Some people like to use form-fillable PDFs on a laptop or tablet computer. Any of that's fine, but you definitely want something that lets you erase and change.

ASPECTS IN A NUTSHELL

An **aspect** is a word, phrase, or sentence that describes something centrally important to your character. It can be a motto your character lives by, a personality quirk, a description of a relationship you have with another character, an important possession or bit of equipment your character has, or any other part of your character that is vitally important.

Establishing setting facts: p. 29

Aspects allow you to change the story in ways that tie in with your character's tendencies, skills, or problems. You can also use them to establish facts about the setting, such as the presence of magic or the existence of a useful ally, dangerous enemy, or secret organization.

Your character will have a handful of aspects (between three and five), including a **high concept** and a **trouble**. We discuss aspects in detail in *Aspects and Fate Points*—but for now, this should help you get the idea.

Aspects and Fate Points: p. 25

HIGH CONCEPT

First, decide on your character's **high concept**. This is a single phrase or sentence that neatly sums up your character, saying who you are, what you do, what your "deal" is. When you think about your high concept, try to think of two things: how this aspect could help you, and how it might make things harder for you. Good high concept aspects do both.

Examples: ***Feline Captain of Cirrus Skimmer***; ***Suncaller of the Andral Desert***; ***Chief Field Agent of IGEMA***

FATE ACCELERATED

TROUBLE

Next, decide on the thing that always gets you into **trouble**. It could be a personal weakness, or a recurring enemy, or an important obligation—anything that makes your life complicated.

Examples: ***Steel Assassins Want Me Dead***; ***Cast Now, Ask Questions Later***; ***Gotta Look Out for My Little Brother***

ANOTHER ASPECT

Now compose another aspect. Think of something really important or interesting about your character. Are they the strongest person in their hometown? Do they carry a mighty sword known through history? Do they talk too much? Are they filthy rich?

OPTIONAL: ONE OR TWO ADDITIONAL ASPECTS

If you wish, you may create one or two more aspects. These aspects might describe your character's relationship with other player characters or with an NPC. Or, like the third aspect you composed above, it might describe something especially interesting about your character.

If you prefer, you can leave one or both of these aspects blank right now and fill them in later, after the game has started.

NAME AND APPEARANCE

Describe your character's appearance and give them a name.

> ### CREATING CHARACTERS: THE 30-SECOND VERSION
>
> 1. Write two aspects (page 25): a high concept and a trouble.
>
> 2. Write another aspect.
>
> 3. Give your character a name and describe their appearance.
>
> 4. Choose approaches (page 18).
>
> 5. Set your refresh to 3.
>
> 6. You may write up to two more aspects and choose a stunt (page 31) if you wish, or you may do that during play.

APPROACHES

Choose your **approaches**.

Approaches are descriptions of *how* you accomplish tasks. Everyone has the same six approaches:

- Careful
- Clever
- Flashy
- Forceful
- Quick
- Sneaky

Each approach is rated with a bonus. Choose one at Good (+3), two at Fair (+2), two at Average (+1), and one at Mediocre (+0). You can improve these later. We talk about what each approach means and how you use them in *How to Do Stuff: Outcomes, Approaches, and Actions*.

What each approach means: p. 18

Your approaches can say a lot about who you are. Here are some examples:

THE LADDER

In Fate, we use a ladder of adjectives and numbers to rate a character's approaches, the result of a roll, difficulty ratings for simple checks, etc.

Here's the ladder:

+8	Legendary
+7	Epic
+6	Fantastic
+5	Superb
+4	Great
+3	Good
+2	Fair
+1	Average
0	Mediocre
-1	Poor
-2	Terrible

- **The Brute:**
  Forceful +3, Careful and Flashy +2, Sneaky and Quick +1, Clever +0

- **The All-Star:**
  Quick +3, Forceful and Flashy +2, Clever and Careful +1, Sneaky +0

- **The Trickster:**
  Clever +3, Sneaky and Flashy +2, Forceful and Quick +1, Careful +0

- **The Guardian:**
  Careful +3, Forceful and Clever +2, Sneaky and Quick +1, Flashy +0

- **The Thief:**
  Sneaky +3, Careful and Quick +2, Clever and Flashy +1, Forceful +0

- **The Swashbuckler:**
  Flashy +3, Quick and Clever +2, Forceful and Sneaky +1, Careful +0

STUNTS AND REFRESH

A **stunt** is a special trait that changes the way an approach works for your character. Generally, stunts give you a bonus (almost always +2) to a certain approach when used with a particular action under specific circumstances. We'll talk more about stunts in *Stunts*. Choose one stunt to start, or you can wait and add a stunt during the game. Later, when your character advances, you can choose more.

Stunts: p. 31

Your **refresh** is the number of fate points you begin each game session with—unless you ended the previous session with more unspent fate points than your refresh, in which case you start with the number you had left last time. By default, your refresh starts at three and is reduced by one for each stunt *after* the first three you choose—essentially, your first three stunts are free! As your character advances, you'll get opportunities to add to your refresh. Your refresh may never go below one.

HOW MANY STUNTS?

By default, *FAE* suggests choosing one stunt to start with.

However, if this is your first time playing a Fate game, you might find it easier to pick your first stunt after you've had a chance to play a bit, to give you an idea of what a good stunt might be. Just add your stunt during or after your first game session.

On the other hand, if you're an experienced Fate gamer, you might look ahead and discover that, just like in *Fate Core*, your character is entitled to three free stunts before it starts costing you refresh. In that case, let the least experienced member of your game group be your guide; if someone is new to the game and only takes one to start with, that's what everyone should do. If you're all experienced, and you want to start with more powerful characters, just take all three to start and off you go.

WHO DO YOU WANT TO BE?

HOW TO DO STUFF: OUTCOMES, ACTIONS, AND APPROACHES

Now it's time to start doing something. You need to leap from one moving train car to another. You need to search the entire library for that spell you really need. You need to distract the guard so you can sneak into the fortress. How do you figure out what happens?

First you narrate what your character is trying to do. Your character's own aspects provide a good guide for what you *can* do. If you have an aspect that suggests you can perform magic, then cast that spell. If your aspects describe you as a swordsman, draw that blade and have at it. These story details don't have additional mechanical impact. You don't get a bonus from your magic or your sword, unless you choose to spend a fate point to **invoke** an appropriate aspect (page 27). Often, the ability to use an aspect to make something true in the story is bonus enough!

How do you know if you're successful? Often, you just succeed, because the action isn't hard and nobody's trying to stop you. But if failure provides an interesting twist in the story, or if something unpredictable could happen, you need to break out the dice.

TAKING ACTION: THE 30-SECOND VERSION

1. Describe what you want your character to do. See if someone or something can stop you.

2. Decide what action you're taking: *create an advantage*, *overcome*, *attack*, or *defend*.

3. Decide on your approach.

4. Roll dice and add your approach's bonus.

5. Decide whether to modify your roll with aspects.

6. Figure out your outcome.

DICE OR CARDS

Part of determining your outcome is generating a random number, which is usually done in one of two ways: rolling four Fate Dice, or drawing a card from a Deck of Fate.

Fate Dice: Fate Dice (sometimes called Fudge dice, after the game they were originally designed for) are one way to determine outcomes. You always roll Fate Dice in a set of four. Each die will come up as ⊟, ■, or ⊞, and you add them together to get the total of the roll. For example:

⊟⊞■⊞ = +1   ⊞⊟■■ = 0

⊞⊞⊞⊟ = +2   ⊟■■■ = −1

Deck of Fate: The Deck of Fate is a deck of cards that copies the statistical spread of Fate Dice. You can choose to use them instead of dice—either one works great.

> These rules are written with the assumption that you're rolling Fate Dice, but use whichever one your group prefers. Anytime you're told to roll dice, that also means you can draw from the Deck of Fate instead.

OUTCOMES

Once you roll your dice, add your approach bonus (we'll talk about that in a moment) and any bonuses from aspects or stunts. Compare the total to a target number, which is either a fixed difficulty or the result of the GM's roll for an NPC. Based on that comparison, your outcome is:

Setting difficulties: p. 37

- You **fail** if your total is *less than* your opponent's total.

- It's a **tie** if your total is *equal to* your opponent's total.

- You **succeed** if your total is *greater than* your opponent's total.

- You **succeed with style** if your total is at least *three greater than* your opponent's total.

Now that we've covered outcomes, we can talk about actions and how the outcomes work with them.

ACTIONS

So you've narrated what your PC is trying to do, and you've established that there's a chance you could fail. Next, figure out what **action** best describes what you're trying to do. There are four basic actions that cover anything you do in the game.

CREATE AN ADVANTAGE

Creating an advantage is anything you do to try to help yourself or one of your friends. Taking a moment to very carefully aim your proton blaster, spending several hours doing research in the school library, or tripping the thug who's trying to rob you—these all count as creating an advantage. The target of your action may get a chance to use the defend action to stop you. The advantage you create lets you do one of the following three things:

More on aspects: p. 25

- Create a new situation aspect.

- Discover an existing situation aspect or another character's aspect that you didn't know about.

- Take advantage of an existing aspect.

If you're creating a new aspect or discovering an existing one:

- **If you fail:** Either you don't create or discover the aspect at all, or you create or discover it but an *opponent* gets to invoke the aspect for free. The second option works best if the aspect you create or discover is something that other people could take advantage of (like ***Rough Terrain***). You may have to reword the aspect to show that it benefits the other character instead of you—work it out in whatever way makes the most sense with the player who gets the free invocation. You can still invoke the aspect if you'd like, but it'll cost you a fate point.

Boosts: p. 26

- **If you tie:** If you're creating a new aspect, you get a **boost**. Name it and invoke it once for free—after that, the boost goes away. If you're trying to discover an existing aspect, treat this as a success (see below).

- **If you succeed:** You create or discover the aspect, and you or an ally may invoke it once for free. Write the aspect on an index card or sticky note and place it on the table.

- **If you succeed with style:** You create or discover the aspect, and you or an ally may invoke it *twice* for free. Usually you can't invoke the same aspect twice on the same roll, but this is an exception; success with style gives you a BIG advantage!

FATE ACCELERATED

If you're trying to take advantage of an aspect you already know about:

- **If you fail:** You don't get any additional benefit from the aspect. You can still invoke it in the future if you'd like, at the cost of a fate point.

- **If you tie or succeed:** You get one free invocation on the aspect for you or an ally to use later. You might want to draw a circle or a box on the aspect's note card, and check it off when that invocation is used.

- **If you succeed with style:** You get *two* free invocations on the aspect, which you can let an ally use, if you wish.

ACTIONS & OUTCOMES: THE 30-SECOND VERSION

Create an Advantage when creating or discovering aspects:
- **Fail:** Don't create or discover, or you do but your opponent (not you) gets a free invocation.
- **Tie:** Get a **boost** if creating new, or treat as success if looking for existing.
- **Succeed:** Create or discover the aspect, get a free invocation on it.
- **Succeed with Style:** Create or discover the aspect, get two free invocations on it.

Create an Advantage on an aspect you already know about:
- **Fail:** No additional benefit.
- **Tie:** Generate one free invocation on the aspect.
- **Succeed:** Generate one free invocation on the aspect.
- **Succeed with Style:** Generate two free invocations on the aspect.

Overcome:
- **Fail:** Fail, or succeed at a serious cost.
- **Tie:** Succeed at minor cost.
- **Succeed:** You accomplish your goal.
- **Succeed with Style:** You accomplish your goal and generate a **boost**.

Attack:
- **Fail:** No effect.
- **Tie:** Attack doesn't harm the target, but you gain a boost.
- **Succeed:** Attack hits and causes damage.
- **Succeed with Style:** Attack hits and causes damage. May reduce damage by one to generate a boost.

Defend:
- **Fail:** You suffer the consequences of your opponent's success.
- **Tie:** Look at your opponent's action to see what happens.
- **Succeed:** Your opponent doesn't get what they want.
- **Succeed with Style:** Your opponent doesn't get what they want, and you get a boost.

OVERCOME

Setting difficulties: p. 37

You use the **overcome** action when you have to get past something that's between you and a particular goal—picking a lock, escaping from handcuffs, leaping across a chasm, flying a spaceship through an asteroid field. Taking some action to eliminate or change

Removing a situation aspect: p. 26

an inconvenient situation aspect is usually an overcome action; we'll talk more about that in *Aspects and Fate Points*. The target of your action may get a chance to use the defend action to stop you.

- **If you fail:** You have a tough choice to make. You can simply fail—the door is still locked, the thug still stands between you and the exit, the enemy spaceship is still *On Your Tail*. Or you can succeed, but at a serious cost—maybe you drop something vital you were carrying, maybe you suffer harm. The GM helps you figure out an appropriate cost.

- **If you tie:** You attain your goal, but at some minor cost. The GM could introduce a complication, or present you with a tough choice (you can rescue one of your friends, but not the other), or some other twist. See *"Succeed at a Cost"* in *Running the Game* in *Fate Core* for more ideas.

- **If you succeed:** You accomplish what you were trying to do. The lock springs open, you duck around the thug blocking the door, you manage to lose the alien spaceship on your tail.

- **If you succeed with style:** As success (above), but you also gain a boost.

ATTACK

Use an **attack** when you try to hurt someone, whether physically or mentally—swinging a sword, shooting a blaster rifle, or yelling a blistering insult with the intent to hurt your target. (We'll talk about this in *Ouch! Damage, Stress, and Consequences*, but the important thing is: If someone gets hurt too badly, they're knocked out of the scene.) The target of your attack gets a chance to use the defend action to stop you.

> Damage, Stress, and Consequences: p. 22

- **If you fail:** Your attack doesn't connect. The target parries your sword, your shot misses, your target laughs off your insult.

- **If you tie:** Your attack doesn't connect strongly enough to cause any harm, but you gain a boost.

- **If you succeed:** Your attack hits and you do damage. See *Ouch! Damage, Stress, and Consequences.*

- **If you succeed with style:** You hit and do damage, plus you have the option to reduce the damage your hit causes by one and gain a boost.

> Doing damage: p. 23

DEFEND

Use **defend** when you're actively trying to stop someone from doing any of the other three actions—you're parrying a sword strike, trying to stay on your feet, blocking a doorway, and the like. Usually this action is performed on *someone else's turn*, reacting to their attempt to attack, overcome, or create an advantage. You may also roll to oppose some non-attack actions, or to defend against an attack on someone else, if you can explain why you can. Usually it's fine if most people at the table agree that it's reasonable, but you can also point to a relevant situation aspect to justify it. When you do, you become the target for any bad results.

- **If you fail:** You're on the receiving end of whatever your opponent's success gives them.

- **If you tie or succeed:** Things don't work out too badly for you; look at the description of your opponent's action to see what happens.

- **If you succeed with style:** Your opponent doesn't get what they want, plus you gain a boost.

GETTING HELP

An ally can help you perform your action. When an ally helps you, they give up their action for the exchange and describe how they're providing the help; you get a +1 to your roll for each ally that helps this way. Usually only one or two people can help this way before they start getting in each other's way; the GM decides how many people can help at once.

OUTCOMES, ACTIONS, AND APPROACHES

CHOOSE YOUR APPROACH

Who Do You
Want to Be?
p. 8

As we mentioned in *Who Do You Want to Be?*, there are six **approaches** that describe how you perform actions.

- **Careful:** A Careful action is when you pay close attention to detail and take your time to do the job right. Lining up a long-range arrow shot. Attentively standing watch. Disarming a bank's alarm system.
- **Clever:** A Clever action requires that you think fast, solve problems, or account for complex variables. Finding the weakness in an enemy swordsman's style. Finding the weak point in a fortress wall. Fixing a computer.
- **Flashy:** A Flashy action draws attention to you; it's full of style and panache. Delivering an inspiring speech to your army. Embarrassing your opponent in a duel. Producing a magical fireworks display.
- **Forceful:** A Forceful action isn't subtle—it's brute strength. Wrestling a bear. Staring down a thug. Casting a big, powerful magic spell.
- **Quick:** A Quick action requires that you move quickly and with dexterity. Dodging an arrow. Getting in the first punch. Disarming a bomb as it ticks 3... 2... 1...
- **Sneaky:** A Sneaky action is done with an emphasis on misdirection, stealth, or deceit. Talking your way out of getting arrested. Picking a pocket. Feinting in a sword fight.

Each character has each approach rated with a bonus from +0 to +3. Add the bonus to your dice roll to determine how well your PC performs the action you described.

So your first instinct is probably to pick the action that gives you the greatest bonus, right? But it doesn't work like that. You have to base your choice of approach on the description of your action, and you can't describe an action that doesn't make any sense. Would you Forcefully creep through a dark room, hiding from the guards? No, that's being Sneaky. Would you Quickly push that big rock out of the way of the wagon? No, that's being Forceful. Circumstances constrain what approach you can use, so sometimes you have to go with an approach that might not play directly to your strengths.

ROLL THE DICE, ADD YOUR BONUS

Time to take up dice and roll. Take the bonus associated with the approach you've chosen and add it to the result on the dice. If you have a stunt that applies, add that too. That's your total. Compare it to what your opponent (usually the GM) has.

Invoking
aspects:
p. 27

DECIDE WHETHER TO MODIFY THE ROLL

Finally, decide whether you want to alter your roll by invoking aspects— we'll talk about this a lot in *Aspects and Fate Points*.

FATE ACCELERATED

CHALLENGES, CONTESTS, AND CONFLICTS

We've talked about the four actions (create an advantage, overcome, attack, and defend) and the four outcomes (fail, tie, succeed, and succeed with style). But in what framework do those happen?

Usually, when you want to do something straightforward—swim across a raging river, hack someone's cell phone—all you need to do is make one overcome action against a difficulty level that the GM sets. You look at your outcome and go from there.

Setting difficulties: p. 37

But sometimes things are a little more complex.

CHALLENGES

A **challenge** is a series of overcome and create an advantage actions that you use to resolve an especially complicated situation. Each overcome action deals with one task or part of the situation, and you take the individual results together to figure out how the situation resolves.

To set up a challenge, decide what individual tasks or goals make up the situation, and treat each one as a separate overcome roll.

Depending on the situation, one character may be required to make several rolls, or multiple characters may be able to participate. GMs, you aren't obligated to announce all the stages in the challenge ahead of time—adjust the steps as the challenge unfolds to keep things exciting.

> The PCs are the crew of a ship caught in a storm. They decide to press on and try to get to their destination despite the weather, and the GM suggests this sounds like a challenge. Steps in resolving this challenge could be calming panicky passengers, repairing damaged rigging, and keeping the ship on the right heading.

CONTESTS

When two or more characters are competing against one another for the same goal, but not directly trying to hurt each other, you have a **contest**. Examples include a car chase, a public debate, or an archery tournament.

A contest proceeds in a series of exchanges. In an exchange, every participant takes one overcome action to determine how well they do in that leg of the contest. Compare your result to everyone else's.

If you got the highest result, you win the exchange—you score a victory (which you can represent with a tally or check mark on scratch paper) and describe how you take the lead. If you succeed with style, you mark two victories.

If there's a tie, no one gets a victory, and an unexpected twist occurs. This could mean several things, depending on the situation—the terrain or environment shifts somehow, the parameters of the contest change, or an unanticipated variable shows up and affects all the participants. The GM creates a new situation aspect reflecting this change and puts it into play.

The first participant to achieve three victories wins the contest.

Situation aspects: p. 26

CONFLICTS

Conflicts are used to resolve situations where characters are trying to harm one another. It could be physical harm (a sword fight, a wizard's duel, a battle with laser blasters), but it could also be mental harm (a shouting match, a tough interrogation, a magical psychic assault).

SETTING THE SCENE

Establish what's going on, where everyone is, and what the environment is like. Who is the opposition? The GM should write a couple of situation aspects on sticky notes or index cards and place them on the table. Players can suggest situation aspects, too.

Situation aspects: p. 26

The GM also establishes **zones**, loosely defined areas that tell you where characters are. You determine zones based on the scene and the following guidelines:

Generally, you can interact with other characters in the same zone—or in nearby zones if you can justify acting at a distance (for example, if you have a ranged weapon or magic spell).

> ### CONFLICTS: THE 30-SECOND VERSION
>
> 1. Set the scene.
>
> 2. Determine turn order.
>
> 3. Start the first exchange.
>
> - On your turn, take an action.
>
> - On other people's turns, defend against or respond to their actions as necessary.
>
> - At the end of everyone's turn, start a new exchange or end the conflict.

FATE ACCELERATED

You can move one zone for free. An action is required to move if there's an obstacle along the way, such as someone trying to stop you, or if you want to move two or more zones. It sometimes helps to sketch a quick map to illustrate zones.

> Thugs are attacking the characters in a house. The living room is one zone, the kitchen another, the front porch another, and the yard a fourth. Anyone in the same zone can easily throw punches at each other. From the living room, you can throw things at people in the kitchen or move into the kitchen as a free action, unless the doorway is blocked. To get from the living room to the front porch or yard requires an action.

DETERMINE TURN ORDER

Your turn order in a conflict is based on your approaches. In a physical conflict, compare your Quick approach to the other participants'—the one with the fastest reflexes goes first. In a mental conflict, compare your Careful approach—attention to detail will warn you of danger. Whoever has the highest approach gets to go first, and then everyone else goes in descending order. Break ties in whatever manner makes sense, with the GM having the last word.

GMs, it's simplest if you pick your most advantageous NPC to determine your place in the turn order, and let all your NPCs go at that time. But if you have a good reason to determine turn order individually for all your NPCs, go right ahead.

EXCHANGES

Next, each character takes a turn in order. On their turn, a character can take one of the four actions. Resolve the action to determine the outcome. The conflict is over when only one side has characters still in the fight.

Four actions: p. 14

CHALLENGES, CONTESTS, AND CONFLICTS

OUCH! DAMAGE, STRESS, AND CONSEQUENCES

When you're hit by an attack, the severity of the hit is the difference between the attack roll and your defense roll; we measure that in **shifts**. For instance, if your opponent gets +5 on their attack and you get a +3 on your defense, the attack deals a two shift hit (5 − 3 = 2).

Then, one of two things happens:

- You suffer **stress** and/or **consequences**, but you stay in the fight.

- You get **taken out**, which means you're out of the action for a while.

STRESS & CONSEQUENCES: THE 30-SECOND VERSION

- Each character starts with three stress boxes.

- Severity of hit (in shifts)
= Attack Roll − Defense Roll

- When you take a hit, you need to account for how that hit damages you. One way to absorb the damage is to take stress; you can check one stress box to handle some or all of a single hit. You can absorb a number of shifts equal to the number of the box you check: one for Box 1, two for Box 2, three for Box 3.

- You may also take one or more consequences to deal with the hit, by marking off one or more consequence slots and writing a new aspect for each one. Mild consequence = 2 shifts; moderate = 4 shifts; severe = 6 shifts.

- If you can't (or decide not to) handle the entire hit, you're taken out. Your opponent decides what happens to you.

- Giving in before your opponent's roll allows you to control how you exit the scene. You also get one or more fate points for doing this!

- Stress and mild consequences vanish at the end of the scene, provided you get a chance to rest. Other consequences take longer.

WHAT IS STRESS?

If you get hit and don't want to be taken out, you can choose to take stress.

Stress represents you getting tired or annoyed, taking a superficial wound, or some other condition that goes away quickly.

Your character sheet has a **stress track**, a row of three boxes. When you take a hit and check a stress box, the box absorbs a number of shifts equal to its number: one shift for Box 1, two for Box 2, or three for Box 3.

You can only check one stress box for any single hit, but you *can* check a stress box and take one or more consequences at the same time. You can't check a stress box that already has a check mark in it!

WHAT ARE CONSEQUENCES?

Consequences are new aspects that you take to reflect being seriously hurt in some way. Your character sheet has three slots where you can write consequences. Each one is labeled with a number: 2 (mild consequence), 4 (moderate consequence), or 6 (severe consequence). This represents the number of shifts of the hit the consequence absorbs. You can mark off as many of these as you like to handle a single hit, but only if that slot was blank to start with. If you already have a moderate consequence written down, you can't take another one until you do something to make the first one go away!

A major downside of consequences is that each consequence is a new aspect that your opponents can invoke against you. The more you take, the more vulnerable you are. And just like situation aspects, the character that creates it (in this case, the character that hit you) gets one free invocation on that consequence. They can choose to let one of their allies use the free invocation.

Let's say that you get hit really hard and take a 4-shift hit. You check Box 2 on your stress track, which leaves you with 2 shifts to deal with. If you can't, you're taken out, so it's time for a consequence. You can choose to write a new aspect in the consequence slot labeled 2—say, **Sprained Ankle**. Those final 2 shifts are taken care of and you can keep fighting!

If you're unable to absorb all of a hit's shifts—by checking a stress box, taking consequences, or both—you're taken out.

WHAT HAPPENS WHEN I GET TAKEN OUT?

If you get taken out, you can no longer act in the scene. Whoever takes you out narrates what happens to you. It should make sense based on how you got taken out—maybe you run from the room in shame, or maybe you get knocked unconscious.

GIVING IN

If things look grim for you, you can **give in** (or **concede** the fight)—but you have to say that's what you're going to do *before* your opponent rolls their dice.

This is different than being taken out, because you get a say in what happens to you. Your opponent gets some major concession from you—talk about what makes sense in your situation—but it beats getting taken out and having no say at all.

Additionally, you get one fate point for conceding, and one fate point for each consequence you took in this conflict. This is your chance to say, "You win this round, but I'll get you next time!" and get a tall stack of fate points to back it up.

GETTING BETTER—RECOVERING FROM STRESS AND CONSEQUENCES

At the end of each scene, clear all of your stress boxes. Recovery from a consequence is a bit more complicated; you need to explain how you recover from it—whether that's an ER visit, taking a walk to calm down, or whatever makes sense with the consequence. You also need to wait an appropriate length of time.

- **Mild consequence:** Clear it at the end of the scene, provided you get a chance to rest.

- **Moderate consequence:** Clear it at the end of the next session, provided it makes sense within the story.

Scenarios: p. 36
- **Severe consequence:** Clear it at the end of the *scenario*, provided it makes sense within the story.

RENAMING MODERATE AND SEVERE CONSEQUENCES

Moderate and severe consequences stick around for a while. Therefore, at some point you may want to change the name of the aspect to better fit what's going on in the story. For instance, after you get some medical help, *Painful Broken Leg* might make more sense if you change it to *Hobbling on Crutches*.

ASPECTS AND FATE POINTS

An **aspect** is a word or phrase that describes something special about a person, place, thing, situation, or group. Almost anything you can think of can have aspects. A person might be the ***Greatest Swordswoman on the Cloud Sea***. A room might be ***On Fire*** after you knock over an oil lamp. After a time-travel encounter with a dinosaur, you might be ***Terrified***. Aspects let you change the story in ways that go along with your character's tendencies, skills, or problems.

You **spend fate points**—which you keep track of with pennies or glass beads or poker chips or some other tokens—to unlock the power of aspects and make them help you. You **earn** fate points by letting a character aspect be compelled against you to complicate the situation or make your life harder. Be sure to keep track of the fate points you have left at the end of the session—if you have more than your refresh, you start the next session with the fate points you ended this session with.

Refresh: p. 11

You earned a lot of fate points during your game session, ending the day with five fate points. Your refresh is 2, so you'll start with five fate points the next time you play. But another player ends the same session with just one fate point. His refresh is 3, so he'll begin the next session with 3 fate points, not just the one he had left over.

WHAT KINDS OF ASPECTS ARE THERE?

There's an endless variety of aspects, but no matter what they're called they all work pretty much the same way. The main difference is how long they stick around before going away.

Character Aspects: These aspects are on your character sheet, such as your high concept and trouble. They describe personality traits, important details about your past, relationships you have with others, important items or titles you possess, problems you're dealing with or goals you're working toward, or reputations and obligations you carry. These aspects only change under very unusual circumstances; most never will.

High concept: p. 8

Trouble: p. 9

Examples: ***Captain of the Skyship Nimbus***; ***On the Run From the Knights of the Circle***; ***Attention to Detail***; ***I Must Protect My Brother***

Situation Aspects: These aspects describe the surroundings that the action is taking place in. This includes aspects you create or discover using the **create an advantage** action. A situation aspect usually vanishes at the end of the scene it was part of, or when someone takes some action that would change or get rid of it. Essentially, they last only as long as the situational element they represent lasts.

Examples: ***On Fire***; ***Bright Sunlight***; ***Crowd of Angry People***; ***Knocked to the Ground***

To get rid of a situation aspect, you can attempt an overcome action to eliminate it, provided you can think of a way your character could accomplish it—dump a bucket of water on the ***Raging Fire***, use evasive maneuvers to escape the enemy fighter that's ***On Your Tail***. An opponent may use a Defend action to try to preserve the aspect, if they can describe how they do it.

Recovery from consequences: p. 24

Consequences: These aspects represent injuries or other lasting trauma that happen when you get hit by attacks. They go away slowly, as described in *Ouch! Damage, Stress, and Consequences.*

Examples: ***Sprained Ankle***; ***Fear of Spiders***; ***Concussion***; ***Debilitating Self-Doubt***

Boosts: A boost is a temporary aspect that you get to use once (see *"What Do You Do With Aspects?"* next), then it vanishes. Unused boosts vanish when the scene they were created in is over or when the advantage they represent no longer exists. These represent very brief and fleeting advantages you get in conflicts with others.

Examples: ***In My Sights***; ***Distracted***; ***Unstable Footing***; ***Rock in His Boot***

FATE ACCELERATED

WHAT DO YOU DO WITH ASPECTS?

There are three big things you can do with aspects: **invoke** aspects, **compel** aspects, and use aspects to **establish facts**.

INVOKING ASPECTS

You **invoke** an aspect to give yourself a bonus or make things a bit harder for your opponent. You can invoke any aspect that you a) know about, and b) can explain how you use it to your advantage—including aspects on other characters or on the situation. Normally, invoking an aspect costs you a fate point—hand one of your fate points to the GM. To invoke an aspect, you need to describe how that aspect helps you in your current situation.

> - I attack the zombie with my sword. I know zombies are **Sluggish**, so that should help me.
> - I really want to scare this guy. I've heard he's **Scared of Mice**, so I'll release a mouse in his bedroom.
> - Now that the guard's **Distracted**, I should be able to sneak right by him.
> - This spell needs to be really powerful—I'm an **Archwizard of the Ancient Order**, and powerful spells are my bread and butter.

PVP

The only time that fate point might not go to the GM is when you're in conflict with another player. If you are, and you invoke one of that player's character aspects to help you out against them, they will get the fate point instead of the GM once the scene is over.

What does invoking the aspect get you? Choose one of the following effects:

- Add a +2 bonus to your total. This costs a fate point.

- Reroll the dice. This option is best if you rolled really lousy (usually a –3 or –4 showing on the dice). This costs a fate point.

- Confront an opponent with the aspect. You use this option when your opponent is trying something and you think an existing aspect would make it harder for them. For instance, an alien thug wants to draw his blaster pistol, but he's **Buried in Debris**; you spend a fate point to invoke that aspect, and now your opponent's level of difficulty is increased by +2.

- Help an ally with the aspect. Use this option when a friend could use some help and you think an existing aspect would make it easier for them. You spend a fate point to invoke the aspect, and now your friend gets a +2 on their roll.

Important: You can only invoke any aspect once on a given dice roll; you can't spend a stack of fate points on one aspect and get a huge bonus from it. However, you *can* invoke several different aspects on the same roll.

If you're invoking an aspect to add a bonus or reroll your dice, wait until *after* you've rolled to do it. No sense spending a fate point if you don't need to!

Succeed with style: p. 13

Boosts: p. 26

Free invocations: Sometimes you can invoke an aspect for free, without paying a fate point. If you create or discover an aspect through the **create an advantage** action, the first invocation on it (by you or an ally) is free (if you succeeded with style, you get *two* freebies). If you cause a consequence through an attack, you or an ally can invoke it once for free. A **boost** is a special kind of aspect that grants one free invocation, then it vanishes.

COMPELLING ASPECTS

If you're in a situation where having or being around a certain aspect means your character's life is more dramatic or complicated, anyone can **compel** the aspect. You can even compel it on yourself—that's called a self-compel. Compels are the most common way for players to earn more fate points.

There are two types of compels.

Decision compels: This sort of compel suggests the answer to a decision your character has to make. If your character is **Princess of Alaria**, for example, you may need to stay to lead the defense of the Royal Alarian Castle rather than fleeing to safety. Or if you have a **Defiant Streak a Mile Wide**, maybe you can't help but mouth off to the Dean of Discipline when he questions you.

FATE ACCELERATED

Event compels: Other times a compel reflects something happening that makes life more complicated for you. If you have *Strange Luck*, of course that spell you're working on in class accidentally turns the dour Potions Master's hair orange. If you *Owe Don Valdeon a Favor*, then Don Valdeon shows up and demands that you perform a service for him just when it's least convenient.

In any case, when an aspect is compelled against you, the person compelling it offers you a fate point and suggests that the aspect has a certain effect—that you'll make a certain decision or that a particular event will occur. You can discuss it back and forth, proposing tweaks or changes to the suggested compel. After a moment or two, you need to decide whether to accept the compel. If you agree, you take the fate point and your character makes the suggested decision or the event happens. If you refuse, you must *pay* a fate point from your own supply. Yes, this means that if you don't have any fate points, you can't refuse a compel!

ESTABLISHING FACTS

The final thing that aspects can do is **establish facts** in the game. You don't have to spend any fate points, roll dice, or anything to make this happen— just by virtue of having the aspect *Ruddy Duck's Pilot*, you've established that your character is a pilot and that you fly a plane named the *Ruddy Duck*. Having the aspect *Mortal Enemy: The Red Ninjas* establishes that the setting has an organization called the Red Ninjas and that they're after you for some reason. If you take the aspect *Sorcerer of the Mysterious Circle*, you not only establish that there's a group of sorcerers called the Mysterious Circle, but that *magic exists in the setting and that you can perform it*.

When you establish facts of the setting this way, make sure you do it in cooperation with other players. If most people want to play in a setting without magic, you shouldn't unilaterally bring magic into it through an aspect. Make sure that the facts you establish through your aspects make the game fun for everyone.

COMPOSING GOOD ASPECTS

When you need to think of a good aspect (we're mainly talking about character and situation aspects here), think about two things:

- How the aspect might help you—when you'd invoke it.

- How it might hurt you—when it would be compelled against you.

For example:

I'll Get You, von Stendahl!

- Invoke this when acting against von Stendahl to improve your chances.
- Get a fate point when your dislike for von Stendahl makes you do something foolish to try to get him.

Hair Trigger Nerves

- Invoke this when being extra vigilant and careful would help you.
- Get a fate point when this causes you to be jumpy and be distracted by threats that aren't really there.

Obviously, your trouble aspect is supposed to cause problems—and thereby make your character's life more interesting and get you fate points—so it's okay if that one's a little more one-dimensional, but other character and situation aspects should be double-edged.

FATE ACCELERATED

STUNTS

Stunts are tricks, maneuvers, or techniques your character has that change how an approach works for your character. Generally this means you get a bonus in certain situations, but sometimes it gives you some other ability or characteristic. A stunt can also reflect specialized, high-quality, or exotic equipment that your character has access to that gives them a frequent edge over other characters.

Approaches: p. 18

There's no definitive list of stunts that you pick from; much like aspects, everyone composes their own stunts. There are two basic templates to guide you in composing your stunts, so you do have something to work from.

The first type of stunt gives you a +2 bonus when you use a certain approach in a certain situation. Use this template:

Because I **[describe some way that you are exceptional, have a cool bit of gear, or are otherwise awesome]**, I get a +2 when I **[pick one: Carefully, Cleverly, Flashily, Forcefully, Quickly, Sneakily] [pick one: attack, defend, create advantages, overcome]** when **[describe a circumstance]**.

For example:

- Because I **am a Smooth Talker**, I get a +2 when I **Sneakily create advantages** when **I'm in conversation with someone**.
- Because I **am a Lover of Puzzles**, I get a +2 when I **Cleverly overcome obstacles** when **I am presented with a puzzle, riddle, or similar conundrum**.
- Because I **am a World-Class Duelist**, I get a +2 when I **Flashily attack** when **engaged in a one-on-one swordfight**.
- Because I **have a Big Kite Shield**, I get a +2 when I **Forcefully defend** when **I use my shield in close combat**.

Sometimes, if the circumstance is especially restrictive, you can apply the stunt to both the create an advantage action *and* the overcome action.

The second type of stunt lets you make something true, do something cool, or otherwise ignore the usual rules in some way. Use this template:

Because I **[describe some way that you are exceptional, have a cool bit of gear, or are otherwise awesome]**, once per game session I can **[describe something cool you can do]**.

For example:

- Because I **am Well Connected**, once per game session I can **find a helpful ally in just the right place**.
- Because I **am Quick on the Draw**, once per game session I can **choose to go first in a physical conflict**.
- Because I **can Run Circles Around a Leopard**, once per game session I can **show up anywhere I want to, provided I could run there, no matter where I started**.

These templates exist to give you an idea of how stunts should be constructed, but don't feel constrained to follow them exactly if you have a good idea. If you'd like to read more about the construction of stunts, see *Skills and Stunts* in *Fate Core*.

GETTING BETTER AT DOING STUFF: CHARACTER ADVANCEMENT

People change. Your skills sharpen as you practice them. Your life experiences accumulate and shape your personality. *Fate Accelerated Edition* reflects that with **character advancement**, which allows you to change your aspects, add or change stunts, and raise your approach bonuses. You do this when your character reaches a milestone.

MILESTONES

Stories in TV shows, comic books, movies, and even video games usually continue from episode to episode, season to season. It took Frodo three big books to take the Ring to the fiery mountain. It took Aang three seasons to defeat the Fire Lord. You get the idea. *FAE* can tell those kinds of stories; you play many game sessions in a row using the same characters—this is often called a **campaign**—and the story builds on itself. But within these long stories, there are shorter story arcs, like single episodes of a TV show or single issues of a comic, where shorter stories are told and wrapped up. *FAE* can do that too, even within a longer campaign.

In *FAE*, we call those wrap-ups **milestones**—whether they're small ones for short stories, or really big ones at the end of many sessions of play. *FAE* recognizes three types of milestones, and each one allows you to change your character in certain ways.

MINOR MILESTONES

A **minor milestone** usually occurs at the end of a session of play, or when one piece of a story has been resolved. Rather than making your character more powerful, this kind of milestone is more about changing your character, about adjusting in response to whatever's going on in the story if you need to. Sometimes it won't really make sense to take advantage of a minor milestone, but you always have the opportunity in case you need to.

After a minor milestone, you can choose to do one (and only one) of the following:

- Switch the ratings of any two approaches.

- Rename one aspect that isn't your high concept.

- Exchange one stunt for a different stunt.

- Choose a new stunt (and adjust your refresh, if you already have three stunts).

Also, if you have a moderate consequence, check to see if it's been around for two sessions. If so, you can clear it.

SIGNIFICANT MILESTONES

Scenarios:
p. 36

A **significant milestone** usually occurs at the end of a scenario or the conclusion of a big plot event (or, when in doubt, at the end of every two or three sessions). Unlike minor milestones, which are primarily about change, significant milestones are about learning new things—dealing with problems and challenges has made your character generally more capable at what they do.

In addition to the benefit of a minor milestone, you also gain *both* of the following:

- If you have a severe consequence that's been around for at least two sessions, you can clear it.

- Raise the bonus of one approach by one.

RAISING APPROACH BONUSES

When you raise the bonus of an approach, there's only one rule you need to remember: you can't raise an approach bonus above Superb (+5).

MAJOR MILESTONES

Major milestones should only occur when something happens in the campaign that shakes it up a lot—the end of a big story arc, the final defeat of a main NPC villain, or any other large-scale change that reverberates around your game world.

These milestones are about gaining more power. The challenges of yesterday simply aren't sufficient to threaten these characters anymore, and the threats of tomorrow will need to be more adept, organized, and determined to stand against them.

Achieving a major milestone confers the benefits of a significant milestone *and* a minor milestone. In addition, you may do *all* of the following:

- Take an additional point of refresh, which you may immediately use to purchase a stunt if you wish.

- Rename your character's high concept (optional).

BEING THE GM

The GM has many responsibilities, such as presenting the conflict to the players, controlling NPCs, and helping everyone apply the rules to the situation in the game.

Let's talk about the GM's jobs.

HELP BUILD CAMPAIGNS

A **campaign** is a series of games you play with the same characters, where the story builds on what happened in earlier sessions. All the players should collaborate with the GM to plan how the campaign will work. Usually this is a conversation among all of you to decide what sort of heroes you want to play, what sort of world you live in, and what sorts of bad guys you'll have. Talk about how serious you want the game to be and how long you want it to last.

- Cat-people sky pirates in flying ships, always on the run from the Royal Navy trying to catch them.
- Magic-wielding desert towns-folk stand against the invading soldiers of the evil Steel Empire.
- Students at a boarding school for magical youth solve mysteries and uncover secrets of their ancient school.

LEARNING HOW TO BE A GM

Being a GM and running games can seem intimidating and difficult at first. It's a skill that takes some practice to master, so don't worry—you'll get better the more you do it. If you'd like to read more about the art of GMing Fate, there are several chapters in the *Fate Core* rules that you should check out: *Running the Game, Scenes, Sessions, and Scenarios,* and *The Long Game* are particularly helpful. *Fate Core* is available for free at *www.evilhat.com*.

BUILD SCENARIOS AND RUN GAME SESSIONS

A **scenario** is one short story arc, the sort of thing you might see wrapped up in one or two episodes of an adventure television show, even if it's a smaller part of a bigger story. Usually you can wrap up a scenario in one to three game sessions, assuming you play for three or four hours at a time. But what is a scenario, and how do you build one?

SCENARIOS

A scenario needs two things: A bad guy with a goal, and a reason the PCs can't ignore it.

Bad guy with a goal: You've probably figured this out already. The campaign's main opposition, or one of his allies, is probably your bad guy.

Something the PCs can't ignore: Now you have to give the PCs a reason to care. Make sure the bad guy's goal is up in the PCs' faces, where they need to do something about it or bad things will happen to them, or to people or things they value.

RUNNING GAME SESSIONS

Now that your bad guy is doing something the PCs will pay attention to, it's time to start them off. Sometimes the best way to do that, especially for the first session of a new story arc, is to put them right in the action. Once the PCs know why they should care about what's going on, you just get out of the way and let them take care of it.

That said, there are a bunch of tasks the GM needs to perform to run the session:

- **Run scenes:** A session is made up of individual scenes. Decide where the scene begins, who's there, and what's going on. Decide when all the interesting things have played out and the scene's over.

- **Adjudicate the rules:** When some question comes up about how to apply the rules, you get final say.

Difficulties: p. 37

- **Set difficulties:** You decide how difficult tasks should be.

- **Play the NPCs:** Each player controls their own character, but you control all the rest, including the bad guys.

- **Keep things moving:** If the players don't know what to do next, it's your job to give them a nudge. Never let things get too bogged down in indecision or because they don't have enough information—do something to shake things up.

- **Make sure everyone has a chance to be awesome:** Your goal isn't to defeat the players, but to challenge them. Make sure every PC gets a chance to be the star once in a while, from the big bad warrior to the little sneaky thief.

FATE ACCELERATED

SETTING DIFFICULTY LEVELS

When another character is opposing a PC, their rolls provide the opposition in a conflict, contest, or challenge. But if there's no active opposition, you have to decide how hard the task is.

Low difficulties are best when you want to give the PCs a chance to show off and be awesome. **Difficulties near their approach ratings** are best when you want to provide tension but not overwhelm them. **High difficulties** are best when you want to emphasize how dire or unusual the circumstances are and make them pull out all the stops.

RULES OF THUMB:

- If the task isn't very tough at all, give it a Mediocre (+0)—or just tell the player they succeed without a roll.

- If you can think of at least one reason why the task is tough, pick Fair (+2).

- If the task is extremely difficult, pick Great (+4).

- If the task is impossibly difficult, go as high as you think makes sense. The PC will need to drop some fate points and get lots of help to succeed, but that's fine.

> **OPTIONAL RULE: APPROACH-RELATED TARGET NUMBERS**
>
> Sometimes being Careful makes things a lot easier; sometimes it just takes too long. The GM may wish to adjust the target number up or down by 1 or 2 depending on whether you choose a fitting or a problematic approach. This makes things a bit more complex, but for some groups it's worth it.

BAD GUYS

When you make a bad guy, you can stat them out exactly like the PCs, with approaches, aspects, stress, and consequences. You should do this for important or recurring bad guys who are intended to give the PCs some real difficulties, but you shouldn't need more than one or two of these in a scenario.

Mooks: Other bad guys are **mooks**—unnamed thugs or monsters or goons that are there to make the PCs' day a little more difficult, but they're designed to be more or less easily swept aside, especially by powerful PCs. Here's how you create their stats:

1. Make a list of what this mook is skilled at. They get a +2 to all rolls dealing with these things.

2. Make a list of what this mook is bad at. They get a –2 to all rolls dealing with these things.

3. Everything else gets a +0 when rolled.

4. Give the mook an aspect or two to reinforce what they're good and bad at, or if they have a particular strength or vulnerability. It's okay if a mook's aspects are really simple.

5. Mooks have zero, one, or two boxes in their stress track, depending on how tough you imagine them to be.

6. Mooks can't take consequences. If they run out of stress boxes (or don't have any), the next hit takes them down.

CYCLOPS HOUSE BULLY
Cyclops House Bully, *Cowardly Without Backup*
Skilled (+2) at: Frightening other students, weaseling out of trouble, breaking things
Bad (-2) at: Planning, studying
Stress: None (first hit takes them out)

STEEL ASSASSIN
Steel Assassin, The Night Is Ours
Skilled (+2) at: Sneaking, ambushing
Bad (-2) at: Standing up to determined opposition
Stress: ☐

SKY SHARK
I'm a Shark, Vulnerable Belly
Skilled (+2) at: Flying, biting
Bad (-2) at: Anything that isn't flying or biting
Stress: ☐☐

Groups of Mooks: If you have a lot of low-level bad guys facing the PCs, you can make your job easier by treating them as a group—or maybe a few groups. Instead of tracking a dozen bad guys, you track three groups of four bad guys each. Each of these groups acts like a single character and has a set of stats just like a single mook would:

1. Choose a couple of things they're skilled at. You might designate "ganging up" as one of the things the group is good at.

2. Choose a couple of things they're not so good at.

3. Give them an aspect.

4. Give them one stress box for every two individuals in the group.

GANG OF THUGS
Axe Handles & Crowbars

Skilled (+2) at: Ganging up, scaring innocent people
Bad (-2) at: Thinking ahead, fighting when outnumbered
Stress: ☐☐ (4 thugs)

Fate Core has a way of handling this, called mobs (see the *"Creating the Opposition"* section of the *Running the Game* chapter in *Fate Core*). Feel free to use that option if you prefer. Note that it may lead to very strong mobs, unless you start with extremely weak mooks—if you want to give your PCs a serious challenge, that could be one way to do it.

EXAMPLE CHARACTERS

Here are four sample characters that you can use as-is or use as inspiration for your own characters.

RETH OF THE ANDRALI RESISTANCE

Reth is 14 years of age. He has dark brown skin and dark hair that he wears in thick dreadlocks. He wears light, loose-fitting clothing and sandals, and he's a skilled martial artist. He's the most powerful Suncaller to be born in generations; he can magically call forth the power of fire. Originally from a town in the vast Andral Desert, he and his friends took a stand against the invading Steel Empire and have been living on the run since.

RETH

High Concept:
  Suncaller of the Andral Desert
Trouble: *Steel Assassins Want Me Dead*
Other Aspects: *My Kung Fu Is The Strongest;*
  Crush On Avasa; I Can Learn from Serio's
  Experience

APPROACHES
Careful: Fair (+2)
Clever: Average (+1)
Flashy: Mediocre (+0)
Forceful: Good (+3)
Quick: Fair (+2)
Sneaky: Average (+1)

STUNTS
Stance of the Defiant Sun: Because I have perfected the Stance of the Defiant Sun, I gain a +2 to Forcefully defend in hand-to-hand combat.

(May take two more stunts without reducing refresh!)

STRESS ☐☐☐

CONSEQUENCES
Mild (2):
Moderate (4):
Severe (6):

REFRESH: 3

FATE ACCELERATED

VOLTAIRE

Voltaire is captain of the *Cirrus Skimmer*, a skyship that roams a vast sea of clouds. She's a cat person, her body a blend of human and feline features. She wears an ostentatious assortment of piratey clothes including a long brown jacket, knee-high boots, a feathered cap, and a basket-hilted cutlass. Being a cat person, she does have the tendency to nod off at odd moments…

VOLTAIRE

High Concept:
Feline Captain of Cirrus Skimmer
Trouble: **Yawn**
Other Aspects: *That? Oh, That's a Decoy; Martin Is a Big Cheat; Sanchez Is the Best First Mate a Ship Could Have*

APPROACHES:

Careful: Average (+1)
Clever: Average (+1)
Flashy: Good (+3)
Forceful: Mediocre (+0)
Quick: Fair (+2)
Sneaky: Fair (+2)

STUNTS

Swashbuckling Swordswoman: Because I am a Swashbuckling Swordswoman, I gain a +2 to Flashy attacks when crossing blades with a single opponent.

(May take two more stunts without reducing refresh!)

STRESS ☐☐☐

CONSEQUENCES

Mild (2):
Moderate (4):
Severe (6):

REFRESH: 3

ABIGAIL ZHAO

Abigail is a student at the School of Sorcery, and a member of Hippogriff House. She has light skin and long black hair with a pink streak. She pushes her luck with her school uniform, adding jewelry, studded belts, and dyed designs to the regulation blouse, trousers, and tie. She's especially adept at enchantments. While she loves showing up those goons in Cyclops House, she does have a tendency to act before thinking.

ABIGAIL ZHAO

High Concept: *Enchantment Specialist of Hippogriff House*
Trouble: *Cast Now, Ask Questions Later*
Other Aspects: *I Hate Those Guys in Cyclops House*; *Sarah Has My Back*; *Dexter Fitzwilliam Is Going Down*

APPROACHES

Careful: Mediocre (+0)
Clever: Fair (+2)
Flashy: Average (+1)
Forceful: Fair (+2)
Quick: Average (+1)
Sneaky: Good (+3)

STUNTS

Teacher's Favorite: Because I am a Teacher's Favorite, once per session I may declare that a helpful teacher arrives in the scene.

(May take two more stunts without reducing refresh!)

STRESS ☐☐☐

CONSEQUENCES

Mild (2):
Moderate (4):
Severe (6):

REFRESH: 3

BETHESDA FLUSHING, PHD

Dr. Flushing is a fellow at the Institute for Gravitical and Electro-Mechanical Advancement (IGEMA), and is one of IGEMA's lead test engineers and field agents. IGEMA is frequently in conflict with agents of various international organizations who seek to steal their technology, take over the world, or both. Gustaf von Stendahl, leader of a shadowy spy agency of uncertain affiliation, is frequently a thorn in her side. Dr. Flushing has bright red hair and is never without several gadgets, including her helicopter pack.

BETHESDA FLUSHING

High Concept: *Chief Field Agent of IGEMA*
Trouble: *I'll Get You, von Stendahl!*
Other Aspects: *My Inventions Almost Always Work. Almost.*; *My Grad Students Come Through, Just Not How I Expect Them To*; *I Trust Dr. Alemieda's Genius*

APPROACHES

Careful: Fair (+2)
Clever: Good (+3)
Flashy: Average (+1)
Forceful: Fair (+2)
Quick: Average (+1)
Sneaky: Mediocre (+0)

STUNTS

Experimental Helo Pack: When I use my Experimental Helo Pack, I gain a +2 bonus to Quickly create an advantage or overcome an obstacle if flying would be both possible and helpful.

Gadgeteer: Because I am a Gadgeteer, once per session I may declare that I have an especially useful device that lets me eliminate one situation aspect.

(May take one more stunt without reducing refresh!)

STRESS ☐☐☐

CONSEQUENCES

Mild (2):
Moderate (4):
Severe (6):

REFRESH: 3

DICE RESULTS (PAGE 18)

Result = Dice Roll + Approach Bonus
+ Bonuses from Stunts
+ Bonuses from Invoked Aspects

OUTCOMES (PAGE 13)

Versus Opponent's Result or Target Number:
- **Fail:** Your Result is lower
- **Tie:** Your Result is equal
- **Success:** Your Result is higher by 1 or 2
- **Success with Style:** Your result is higher by 3 or more

SETTING TARGET NUMBERS (PAGE 37)

- **Easy Task:** Mediocre (+0)—or success without a roll.
- **Moderately Difficult:** Fair (+2).
- **Extremely Difficult:** Great (+4).
- **Impossibly Difficult:** Go as high as you think makes sense. The PC will need to drop some fate points and get lots of help to succeed, but that's fine.

THE LADDER

+8	Legendary
+7	Epic
+6	Fantastic
+5	Superb
+4	Great
+3	Good
+2	Fair
+1	Average
0	Mediocre
-1	Poor
-2	Terrible

ACTIONS (PAGE 14)

Create an advantage when creating or discovering aspects (page 14):
- **Fail:** Don't create or discover, or you do but your opponent (not you) gets a free invocation.
- **Tie:** Get a boost if creating new, or treat as success if looking for existing.
- **Succeed:** Create or discover the aspect, get a free invocation on it.
- **Succeed with Style:** Create or discover the aspect, get two free invocations on it.

Create an advantage on an aspect you already know about (page 15):
- **Fail:** No additional benefit.
- **Tie:** Generate one free invocation on the aspect.
- **Succeed:** Generate one free invocation on the aspect.
- **Succeed with Style:** Generate two free invocations on the aspect.

Overcome (page 16):
- **Fail:** Fail, or succeed at a serious cost.
- **Tie:** Succeed at minor cost.
- **Succeed:** You accomplish your goal.
- **Succeed with Style:** You accomplish your goal and generate a boost.

Attack (page 17):
- **Fail:** No effect.
- **Tie:** Attack doesn't harm the target, but you gain a boost.
- **Succeed:** Attack hits and causes damage.
- **Succeed with Style:** Attack hits and causes damage. May reduce damage by one to generate a boost.

Defend (page 17):
- **Fail:** You suffer the consequences of your opponent's success.
- **Tie:** Look at your opponent's action to see what happens.
- **Succeed:** Your opponent doesn't get what they want.
- **Succeed with Style:** Your opponent doesn't get what they want, and you get a boost.

Getting Help (page 17):
- An ally can help you perform your action.
- When an ally helps you, they give up their action for the exchange and describe how they help.
- You get a +1 for each ally that helps in this way.
- GM may place limits on how many may help.

TURN ORDER (PAGE 21)

- **Physical Conflict:** Compare Quick approaches—the one with the fastest reflexes goes first.
- **Mental Conflict:** Compare Careful approaches—the one with the most attention to detail senses danger.
- **Everyone else goes in descending order.** Break ties in whatever manner makes sense, with the GM having the last word.
- **The GM may choose to have all NPCs go on the turn of the most advantageous NPC.**

STRESS & CONSEQUENCES
(PAGE 22)

- **Severity of hit (in shifts)** = Attack Roll − Defense Roll
- **Stress Boxes:** You can check **one** stress box to handle some or all of the shifts of a single hit. You can absorb a number of shifts equal to the number of the box you check: one for Box 1, two for Box 2, three for Box 3.
- **Consequences:** You many take **one or more** consequences to deal with the hit, by marking off one or more available consequence slots and writing a new aspect for each one marked.
  - **Mild** = 2 shifts
  - **Moderate** = 4 shifts
  - **Severe** = 6 shifts
- **Recovering from Consequences:**
  - **Mild consequence:** Clear it at end of the scene.
  - **Moderate consequence:** Clear it at the end of the next session.
  - **Severe consequence:** Clear it at the end of the scenario.
- **Taken Out:** If you can't (or decide not to) handle the entire hit, you're taken out and your opponent decides what happens to you.
- **Giving In:** Give in before your opponent's roll and you can control how you exit the scene. You earn one or more fate points for giving in (page 24).

APPROACHES (PAGE 18)

- **Careful:** When you pay close attention to detail and take your time to do the job right.
- **Clever:** When you think fast, solve problems, or account for complex variables.
- **Flashy:** When you act with style and panache.
- **Forceful:** When you use brute strength.
- **Quick:** When you move quickly and with dexterity.
- **Sneaky:** When you use misdirection, stealth, or deceit.

ASPECTS (PAGE 25)

- **Invoke (page 27):** Spend a fate point to get a +2 or a reroll for yourself, or to increase difficulty for a foe by 2.
- **Compel (page 28):** Receive a fate point when an aspect complicates your life.
- **Establish facts (page 29):** Aspects are true. Use them to affirm details about you and the world.

TYPES OF ASPECTS
Character Aspects (page 25)
- Written when you create your character.
- May be changed when you reach a milestone (page 33).

Situation Aspects (page 26)
- Established at the beginning of a scene.
- May be created by using the create an advantage action.
- May be eliminated by using the overcome action.
- Vanish when the situation ends.

Boosts (page 26)
- May be invoked once (for free), then they vanish.
- May be eliminated by an opponent using an overcome action.
- Unused boosts vanish at the end of the scene.

Consequences (page 23)
- Used to absorb shifts from successful attacks.
- May be invoked by your opponents as if they were situation aspects.

INDEX

Thanks to our feedback heroes, *Fate Accelerated Edition* is the best it can possibly be:
    Andrew Shore, Brian Hoffmann, Carrie Ulrich, Christopher Allen -- RPGnet, Christopher
    Ruthenbeck, Craig Hargraves, Daniel Paarmann, Dataweaver, David Hoberman, Devon Apple,
    Fenikso, Jack Gulick, Jan Stals, Jared Nuzzolillo, Javier Gaspoz, Jay Elmore, John Donoghue,
    Jonathon Hodges, Lisa Padol, Lucian, Mark Gizmo, Mark Watson, Marko Wenzel, Markus Wagner,
    Martín Van Houtte, Mitch A. Williams, Ron Blessing, Wojciech Gebczyk

ID

Name

Description

FATE
ACCELERATED

Refresh

Current Fate Points

ASPECTS

High Concept

Trouble

APPROACHES

CAREFUL

CLEVER

FLASHY

FORCEFUL

QUICK

SNEAKY

STUNTS

STRESS

1 **2** **3**

CONSEQUENCES

2 Mild

4 Moderate

6 Severe